HOVERING HUMMINGBIRDS

by Judith Jango-Cohen

PULL AHEAD BOOKS
Animals

Lerner Publications Company • Minneapolis

Dedicated to my daughter Jennifer, the ballerina, who is as lovely and lively as a hummingbird.

This book is available in two editions:
Library binding by Lerner Publications Company, a division of Lerner Publishing Group, Inc.
Soft cover by First Avenue Editions, an imprint of Lerner Publishing Group, Inc.
241 First Avenue North
Minneapolis, MN 55401

Website address: www.lernerbooks.com

Words in *italic* type are explained in a glossary on page 30.

Library of Congress Cataloging-in-Publication Data

Jango-Cohen, Judith.
    Hovering hummingbirds / by Judith Jango-Cohen.
      p.   cm. — (Pull ahead books)
    Summary: Describes the physical characteristics,
behavior, habitat, and life cycle of hummingbirds.
    ISBN: 978–0–8225–4666–5 (lib. bdg. : alk. paper)
    ISBN: 978–0–8225–3649–9 (pbk. : alk. paper)
    1. Hummingbirds—Juvenile literature.
[1. Hummingbirds.] I. Title. II. Series.
QL696.A558 J36 2003
598.7'64—dc21   2002006598

Manufactured in the United States of America
3 — CG — 5/1/13

Have you ever heard a hummingbird?

Whizzz!
Zzzip!
Zzzing!

A hummingbird sings
with its wings.

It beats its wings so fast
the wind whizzes past.

This tiny flier makes a big sound.

Hummers are tiny birds.
But they are tricky fliers.

They can zip backwards,
and they can flip over.

Hummingbirds can even *hover*.
Beating their wings, they float
in the air.

Why do hummers need to hover?

Hovering hummingbirds can feed
from flowers.

They hover like bees.
Buzzz . . . zzzing!

Hummers feed on *nectar* deep inside flowers.

How do you think they reach this sweet drink?

Hummingbirds reach into flowers
with their long beaks.

Then they lick the sweet nectar
with their quick tongues.

Their tongues flick in and out
of flowers.

Bugs on the flowers
get licked up too.

Some hummingbirds live
where it is warm.

Flowers bloom and bugs buzz
all year long.

But some hummers live where the fall and winter are cold.

Then flowers and bugs die.
What do these hummers do?

In the fall, these hummers *migrate*.
They move to a warmer place.

Males migrate first.
Then females follow.

Do you know how to tell a male
hummingbird from a female?

Most males have *iridescent* feathers on their throats.

Iridescent feathers glitter like pretty bits of glass.

Female hummingbirds are not as pretty as the males.

But they have a big job to do.

A female gathers grass, moss, and bark.

Then she weaves a neat little cup with her beak and feet.

She glues her nest with sticky spiderwebs.

Then she fills the cup with fluff from seeds like silky milkweed.

Soon the female lays two small, white eggs.

She warms the eggs
for about two weeks.

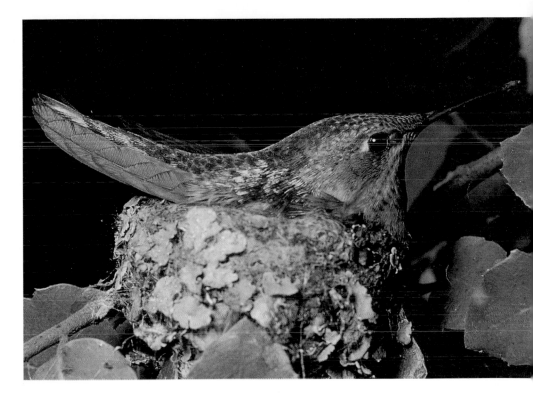

At times she hovers over them and
turns them with her beak.

A female must protect her nest from *predators*.

Predators hunt and eat hummingbird eggs and chicks.

Hummers use their best flying tricks to stay safe.

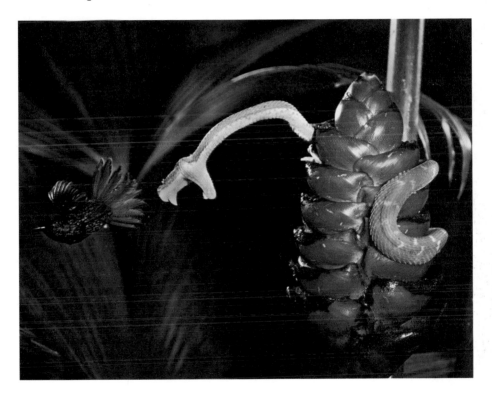

Females protect their nests from squirrels and slinky snakes.

After a few weeks, the tiny hummingbirds hatch.

Mothers catch bugs for their skinny chicks to eat.

Mothers also feed their chicks
sips of sweet nectar.

One day a chubby chick
sits near its nest.

It beats its wings fast
and tries to hover.

Soon it will join the other busy birds of summer.

Whizzz! Zzzip! Zzzing!

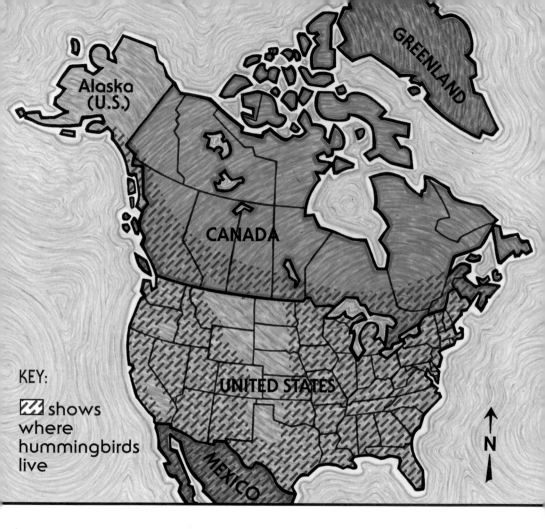

KEY:

shows where hummingbirds live

Find your state or province on this map.
Do hummingbirds live near you?

Parts of a Hummingbird's Body

tongue

beak eye

head

iridescent
feathers

wing

tail

foot

claw

Glossary

hover: to float in one place in the air

iridescent: glittering brightly. A male hummingbird's iridescent feathers shine with the colors of the rainbow.

migrate: to move from one area to another when the seasons change

nectar: the sweet liquid found in flowers

predators: animals that hunt and eat other animals

Index

chicks, 24–26

drinking nectar, 9, 11

eggs, 20–21, 22

hovering, 7–8

nests, 18–19

predators, 22–23

tongues, 10–11

wings, 4–5, 7, 26

About the Author

Eliot Cohen

Sometimes when Judith Jango-Cohen is walking in the woods, she hears a buzz and sees a blur. Then she has the exciting surprise of watching a hummingbird. If you like watching hummers too, buy a hummingbird feeder and see who shows up. Maybe some of the beautiful birds in this book will come to your backyard!

Photo Acknowledgments

The photographs in this book are reproduced with the permission of: © Joe McDonald/Visuals Unlimited, front cover, pages 14, 22; © Garry Walter/Visuals Unlimited, page 3; © Larry Kimball/Visuals Unlimited, page 5; © Barbara Gerlach/Visuals Unlimited, page 13; © Gary W. Carter/Visuals Unlimited, page 18; © John D. Cunningham/Visuals Unlimited, page 21; © G. C. Kelley, Photo Researchers, pages 4, 7, 27, 31; © M. H. Sharp, Photo Researchers, pages 9, 17; © Robert Lee, Photo Researchers, page 10; © Ray Coleman, Photo Researchers, page 11; © Jany Sauvanet, Photo Researchers, page 12; © Anthony Mercieca Photo, Photo Researchers, pages 15, 25; © Richard R. Hansen, Photo Researchers, page 26; © Eileen Herrling/Cornell Laboratory of Ornithology, page 6; © Joe McDonald/CORBIS, page 8; © George D. Lepp/CORBIS, pages 20, 24; © Michael & Patricia Fogden/CORBIS, page 23; © Rob Curtis/The Early Birders, page 16; © Judith Jango-Cohen, page 19.